HOPE DEFINED

HOPE DEFINED

LEARNING TO LIVE WITH THE LOSS OF A LOVED ONE.
FINDING HOPE IN ALL OF THE GOOD THINGS
GOD HAS PLACED IN YOUR LIFE.
HOW I SURVIVED MY MOMS SUICIDE WITH GOD'S HELP

LESLIE STICKEL

Outskirts Press, Inc.
Denver, Colorado

Hope Defined
Learning to live with the loss of a loved one. Finding hope in all of the good things God has placed in your life. How I survived my moms suicide with God's help

v2.0

Outskirts Press, Inc.
http://www.outskirtspress.com

ISBN: 978-1-4327-5334-4

PRINTED IN THE UNITED STATES OF AMERICA

To Patrick, Emily and Samuel
My heart bursts with love for you.
Sometimes I still can't believe God gave you to me. You are my most precious blessings. Thank you for loving me unconditionally. Thank you for speaking nothing but encouraging words to me as I struggled through the process of writing. You bring me joy. Enjoy life….go home!

To my sister, Kristen
You are beautiful.
You are strong.
You are loved.
You are hope defined.
I am so proud of you.

ACKNOWLEDGMENTS

Diane
Julie
Mary
Teri
Linda
Charli

I have been blessed with the most wonderful friends in the world. Each of you is a gift to me, placed in my life at just the right time. You are strong beautiful women of God and I am humbled by your character and wisdom. You are a reflection of Christ for me. I do not know what I would have done without you. Thank you for holding me up, laughing with me, crying with me, praying for me.

Harvest and Shawna thank you for the encouragement. It's been beautiful >

Ken, yer the best boss!

Special thanks to Faye Higbee, your help was invaluable!

Table of Contents

PREFACE 1
1 SHATTERED 5
2 YOU CARRIED ME 9
3 PAT 15
4 MOM AND I 25
5 BOUNDARIES 37
6 AGREE TO DISAGREE 39
7 LAST VISIT 41
8 THE LAST STRAW 45
9 YOUR VOICE 49
10 GRIEF THE UNINVITED GUEST 55
11 ACCEPTANCE, IT'S JUST AN EARTH SUIT 65
12 UNIVERSAL, YET UNIQUE 69
13 A COMMON THREAD 75
14 THE CHURCH FAMILY 81
15 THE MASKS WE WEAR 87
16 EVERYTHING IN MODERATION 91
17 FORGO NORMAL 93
18 KIDS 97
19 COUNT YOUR BLESSINGS 105
20 TALK YOURSELF INTO IT 111
21 TRUST IN THE LORD? 115

22 FAST FORWARD 119
23 SPECIAL DELIVERY 123
24 HOPE 127

PREFACE

I've been compelled to write. Enduring a loss has changed my life. It has changed my perspective on nearly everything. I have a clearer understanding of Grace and I've been able to look at people with something other than my eyes. I have more patience for strangers and I feel more deeply in tune with the pain that is all around me. In the weeks after my loss I would pass people on the street and wonder if they could see how broken I was, which caused me to realize, I am likely not passing anyone at any time that has not felt broken. You have suffered a loss as everyone eventually does. I can't say that what I write will make your loss any easier or help the pain to subside. I am not eloquent with words or necessarily gifted with wisdom. I am not an expert on grief. My hope is that you will know that you are not alone. Loss is not unique to you only. There is no way to measure whose loss is greater, but evidence that we will all face it as sure as the sun sets. What you do with the loss and how it affects your relationship with Christ will make all the difference in who you become through it. God's grace is with you as you read. I pray He holds you close and shines light into your world, your circumstance.

Ultimately, the hope of all He has to offer you will become clearer and guide you.

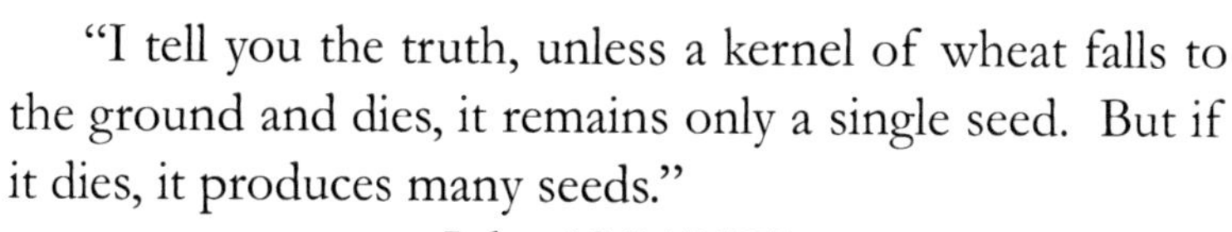

"I tell you the truth, unless a kernel of wheat falls to the ground and dies, it remains only a single seed. But if it dies, it produces many seeds."

John 12:24 NIV

1

SHATTERED

"I can do everything through him who gives me strength"

Philippians 4:13 ®NIV

I remember a crisp, sunny November day so clearly. My husband, Patrick and I looked forward to Saturday morning coffee together. It is a tradition we anticipated as the week progressed. It gave us time to catch up on the week's events and regroup. Feeling particularly lazy, I let Pat make the coffee. I lingered in bed until I could smell the comforting aroma. Stretching and yawning, I slid out of bed half heartedly. I grabbed the faux fur throw blanket and snuggled up on the couch in my snowflake pajamas. With sleepy eyes I gazed out the picture window. It's my favorite view from our house. It overlooks what friends call "peaceful nothingness". It's my own personal view of a golden ocean, endless wheat fields.

I remember feeling very cozy, looking forward to my first sip of hot coffee and the company of my husband. Pat brought me my cup and the phone rang. He picked up the phone and I remember thinking, *what a vague, short conversation.* Pat hung up the phone and walked toward me. As he reached for my coffee to take it from my hands, I saw anguish on his face in the purest form.

"Sweetheart, I'm so sorry. She did it. She's gone baby, your mom shot herself last night."

Torture screamed through my body. I crawled over the back of the couch and ran out the front door. The air pierced my skin. My spirit tried to claw its way out to escape the worst pain I had ever felt. I stumbled around the yard moaning and sobbing, "No mom, mamma no!" I wet myself. I couldn't stop the shaking, the chaos in my mind. When I reflect on that day it's like I was hovering above some scene in a movie, watching the main character try to escape a crazed stalker. I can recall every ache, every involuntary jerk of my body. There was panic and an uncontrollable desire to flee, but I was handcuffed to a horrible writhing monster.

Soaked from my own urine and from falling on the ground, I had no strength to stand. Pat picked me up like a child who had fallen and scrapped her knee. He wrapped a towel around me and sat me in our car. I remember rocking back and forth, my knuckles white from holding myself tightly.

With my face in his hands my husband said, "Leslie, look at me! Look at my eyes! You can't leave. Do you understand? You cannot leave me. I need you too much. I love you so much."

I managed to say, 'OK, I won't' and the name of Jesus found its way to my lips.

I begged, "Jesus, please Jesus be with me. I need You. I'm so afraid. Don't let me go."

Faintly whispered I heard, "Leslie, this will not define you. I will define you. Hope in all that is good will define you. I've got you, do not be afraid."

Diary entry; *Oh God I'm sick. I'm scared. Did I fail? Mom why! I'm so very, very tired.*

Did you really do it? How could you? Didn't you think about us once? You couldn't have thought of the kids, my Emily and Sam that would have stopped you. You've destroyed Kristen!

Oh God help me!

2

YOU CARRIED ME

"Carry each other's burdens, and in this way you will fulfill the law of Christ."

Galatians 6:2 ®NIV

Pat called my closest friend first. Teri and her husband Jeff came as soon as they could. I was walking on the summer road that splits my golden ocean when they arrived. Pat did not want me to take a walk, but I felt like I had to get out, if not of my own skin, at least the house. I knew while I shuffled on that dirt road a set of binoculars was likely on me.

The need to walk may have been part of a desperate need to flee, but it turned out to be the beginning of a new walk I would be taking with the Lord. I began with a shot of adrenaline. It had only been hours since I found out about mom, but rage engulfed me. The river banks of my self-control had been hit by a tsunami and washed away.

With my teeth gritted I growled every foul word known to mankind. I reached the top of the hill and stopped there. One because I promised Pat I would not go out of sight and two because I don't think my legs would have taken me any further, though I wanted them to. I remember thinking, *I wish the other side of this hill dropped off and I could disappear from everything.* On this hill, exhaustion set in. I wanted to collapse in the mud and cry until I fell asleep.

I could hear Pat saying, "What if you fall and can't get up? I don't want you to go".

With tears stinging my red swollen cheeks I whispered, "I can't fall down. I have to get home. I don't think I can get myself home. You are going to have to do it. Lord

God, Please get me home." Slowly, but surely my legs moved. On the longest walk of my life, I mimicked Tim Conway shuffling along in a Carol Burnett skit.

That walk mirrored my relationship with Christ. I simply cannot get home without Him.

As I approached the house my friend Teri met me on the street with a blanket. She wrapped it around me, held me and wept with me. Teri, who is a little woman, bore my weight and got me to the front door, where my husband stood anxiously waiting.

They sat me on the couch, tucked a blanket around me and Teri promptly began making me a cup of tea. She lit candles around the house and cleaned the kitchen. Her husband went almost unnoticed while at our house. Quietly he wrapped a blanket around me when a moment of panic once again had me running out the front door. He embraced my husband. He left a gift on the counter reminding me he kept me in prayer.

They gently moved through our home loving us. For months following, they continued to move through our lives, praying, crying with us, serving us, and displaying grace.

Teri later told me, my situation helped her more fully understand what Christ meant when he told us to carry one another's burdens.

It is a humbling experience to be served by people when you are broken. To watch how life is orchestrated around you and to know they are doing for you what

Christ calls them to. Awesome is the only word.

Those closest to me kept a watchful eye. Friends checked in on me frequently. As time passed, support came in small quiet ways, surprising me the most. For instance, one of my co-workers had the anniversary of my mom's death on her calendar. She wanted to remind herself to be more sensitive towards me in November. Another woman I work with gave me a card on mother's day just to let me know she thought of me. I have a special friend I work with who would come by every few days and give me a hug. She would look at me with a knowing smile and hug me. These acts of kindness comforted me deeply, the ones that lingered.

Friends gave me permission to be broken. They would encourage me to talk, cry or do whatever I felt like doing. It is embarrassing, however, to be perfectly fine one minute and the next, wanting to destroy a set of dishes. My friends encouraged me, "Just do it! We'll watch or help you throw and clean up when you are done. Whatever you need, we are here for you."

My incredible friend Julie said to me, "You are doing great. Believe it or not, you are amazing me. No one knows how someone makes it through something like this, but you are doing it well. There isn't a right way. Don't put too much pressure on yourself to be 'cured' of your grief. This is going to take a very long time and that's ok."

When she said this it was as if I was buried in an avalanche and she was the first one there with a shovel. The pressure I felt from within to get over it lessened.

Although a deafening sorrow in my heart seemed ever present, I could feel the constant prayers for me. Grieving is personal and can be a very lonely place; God and His people carried me through.

My dad took the first flight he could to come and be with my sister and me. He had a tag along, my 89 year old grandpa. My parents divorced when I was 10 and we moved away almost immediately. Therefore, time with my grandpa had been sparse. He has been a man I have always liked. I enjoy his company and find his short edgy way charming. My conversations with him were always brief. "I love you", not something he said back and hugs seemed a bit uncomfortable.

But I refer to the time with my grandpa as my saving grace. My dad stayed with my sister and grandpa stayed in our guest room. From the moment he woke until the moment he headed to bed, he talked with me. He told me stories about his childhood. He talked about his parents and about my dad as a kid. He told me about losses he experienced and cried with me.

He made me laugh, which shocked my system as I think I had decided this would never happen again.

With ease, my grandpa told me he loved me and hugged me. I will forever be grateful to God for the gift of time with him. He loved and looked after me as his grandchild, something I missed and didn't even know it. Grandpa, thank you.

Diary entry; *I laughed today. It felt like I was fumbling my way through a foreign language. I want to drink. I want to drink an entire bottle of wine…maybe two. I'd like to smash an entire set of dishes against the wall of the shed. I hate you so much for doing this to everyone! You are a selfish bitch!*

3

PAT

"Husbands, love your wives, just as Christ loved the church, and gave himself up for her to make her holy, cleansing her by the washing with water through the word, and to present her to himself as a radiant church, without stain or wrinkle or any other blemish, but holy and blameless."

Ephesians 5:25 ®NIV

I married a wonderful, blue eyed, Irish boy, who had been raised Catholic. As an altar boy, he made his mom very proud, which added to her hope he would one day become a priest. God had different plans for Patrick; he placed me smack in the middle of his path.

Raised without church, I had designed my own God. Taught by my mom to believe, God was happy if I was happy. My altar was a closet full of clothing. I took my mom's one time advice and didn't take God stuff too seriously.

Pat took a gigantic leap of faith when he married me. My husband and I debated life's moral issues throughout the first year of our marriage. He was pro-life and I, pro-choice. I believed in the death penalty, he did not. Often Pat looked completely exasperated, his brow furrowed and shoulders slumped like a prize fighter who threw in the towel.

Pat and I had a daughter, Emily, within the first year of our marriage. I thought we had a pretty nice routine on Sundays. He would wake up early and go to Mass. I would stay home, content to make my husband a nice breakfast upon his return or sleep in if Emily was willing.

One Saturday evening Pat came to me with tears in his blue eyes, "I know you aren't really into the idea of church, but I want my kids to grow up knowing God and experiencing church. Would you please consider coming with me on Sundays?"

Sympathetically I said, "Sure, I'll give it a try, if it means that much to you."

However, inside I was a child throwing herself to the ground, *I don't want to go! I don't like church. It's boring and I gotta get up early.*

I don't like church. It's boring and I gotta get up early. I don't understand half the stuff. I don't know any of the songs! I don't know when to sit or stand AND I don't get to have snack when everyone else does!

Pat looked like a little boy showing off his first place trophy. His eyes twinkling and relief relaxed in his cheeks. Through gritted teeth, I smiled back.

Sunday morning came all too soon. I sluggishly got myself ready and pouted my way to the car. As we drove I blurted out, "I'm nervous! I get confused during Mass. I have a hard time understanding what the guy is saying and I don't get to have snack with everyone."

"Communion, the snack is communion. Don't worry, I'll help you. If after today, you want to try other churches, we can."

The following Sunday we attended Life Center, a Four Square church. I saw people laughing and visiting, it felt comfortable. There was a big screen with the words to the songs on it. The man on the stage made the stories in the Bible come to life with modern day connections. I thought, *I could get use to this. It is not so bad —decent music, nice person talking about helpful stuff, people are kind and I get to go up and have snack like everyone else.*

Three Sundays into our new church going lives we

took our seats. I noticed a woman seated five rows in front of us. Her shoulders were shaking and her hands were trembling. She kept wiping her eyes. Every few moments I could hear a mumbled sob.

My heart softened as I watched her. Promptly I had a thought, which seemed to have a life of its own, "You need to go to her. Tell her your name. Tell her everything is going to be fine and you will pray for her."

I argued, "I am not going to go do that. I do not know how to pray!"

"Go to her. Tell her your name. Tell her everything is going to be fine and you will pray for her."

I battled this thought for the course of the sermon, perplexed to be having such a strange idea. When the sermon ended, I got up and started towards the woman.

Confused my husband shouted, "Where are you going?"

"Apparently, I am going up there. I'll be right back."

I arrived at the woman just as she stood up. There we were, toe to toe, she with puffy eyes, swollen red face and snot on her nose. I with sweat beading on my forehead and hands shoved anxiously in my pockets. I stammered, "Hi. I'm Leslie. Everything is going to be fine and I will pray for you." She just stared back at me for an uncomfortable second and said nothing.

"Ok", I said and turned away. I quickly bobbed and weaved my way to the nursery.

Impatiently I waited in line for my child. I planned on

grabbing Emily and making a run for the car! With her in one hand and macaroni art in the other, my escape was near, but then I felt a tap on my shoulder. I turned around and there she was.

She mustered up a smile and said, "I'm sorry I didn't say anything to you. You shocked me. My daughter ran away last night. Her name is Leslie. When you told me your name and that everything was going to be fine and you would pray for me, I knew God used you to speak to me. Thank you for listening to Him and coming to me. I feel so much more peace about the situation."

I am sure I looked pretty much the same way she did when I approached her, minus the tears and snot. Paralyzed by the goose bumps all over my body, "Wow" is all I could come up with.

She hugged me and I left the church at a much slower pace than initially planned.

I was blind and now I can see! I experienced instantaneous transformation of my heart. I had been living in a dark room, no lights, and no windows, suddenly there was light!

I shook my head as truth flooded me and softly I breathed in an understanding for my husband.

I got into the car and before pulling out of the parking lot, eagerly told my husband the entire story.

Patrick let out a loud laugh. His smile from ear to ear sent tears streaming down my cheeks. He leaned over and kissed me, "I'm so happy for you." He whispered, and we drove away from the church.

God is so amazing! He knows each of us so intimately. God knew and still knows how to reach me. He romances me and puts me in a state of awe. He grabbed my attention and boldly made me a part of a relationship with someone I didn't even know existed.

From one's pain came another's salvation! In an instant, he changed my heart and taught me more than I had learned in a lifetime. Our faith truly only has to be the size of a mustard seed. The seed planted in me, so small, I did not even know it existed.

That day likely saved my marriage. It surely saved my life. Without God, I feel confident we would not have made it. Without God, my mom's suicide would have crushed my existence. Without God, Patrick would not have had the strength to sustain him through taking care of me.

My husband was a force field around me at all times. For a few weeks I had, in a way, dropped out of life. I tried to be "fine" and I tried to carry on, but the fact is when the body takes on such a tragedy it needs time to recover from the shock of it all. My mind had been through a trauma and I couldn't focus. I'm normally a fairly active person, but I became pretty sedentary. My mom's suicide, constant in my mind, caused me to turn on the TV for a way to check out. For weeks I fumbled through my days.

Normally a conscientious person, I became oblivious. I would muster up the energy to vacuum, but then never put the vacuum away. I'd just walk over it and around it for several days. I would start a load of laundry and let it sit wet in the washer for days. Pat picked up a lot of slack. He took care of the home, the kids and me. Tenderly he protected me, served me and loved me.

Sometimes I would cry, needy as an infant and other times, withdraw into my pain. I had brief windows when pain did not consume me. I would look at my husband and see a recipe of anger, pain, sympathy, rage, helplessness and exhaustion simmering in his eyes. However, his disposition was so calm and his focus on loving his family with strength that could not possibly have been his own.

I asked Pat, 'How are you?'

I do not see tears from him very often, but tears did brace themselves in his eyes as he said, "I'm not doing very well. I'm worried about you and this whole thing….I just can't believe it.

I'm so sorry baby. I feel like I didn't tell you right or like you could be upset with me for the way I told you about your mom. I just didn't know what to do!"

I love him with all my heart. This wonderful man, who had to tell me my mom took her life. How do you tell someone something like that?

Shaking my head and exhaling a deep breath, I thanked him for loving me so much. I told him he did the best he could and I was not angry with him at all. We clung to each other and sobbed. I could feel the burden melt off of him.

My husband and I grew closer. Without a doubt, he has seen me at my most vulnerable state and he made me feel nothing but safe and protected. I simply cannot describe the power I feel surrounding our love. Our love is stronger as a direct result of this tragedy. I felt terrible for what he had experienced. I would change how we came to this point in our union, but we are better for it. The recipe I saw brewing in his eyes, a passion to love and serve his family stirred by God.

Diary entry; *God, thank you for being my friend. I don't know what you have in mind for all of this hope defined stuff. I'm not a crafty person, but you got me making necklaces, brooches. What are you thinking? Write a book? You do remember who I am right? Can I glorify you with all the garbage floating around my heart? I'm tired. It seems like I always feel tired these days.*

4

MOM AND I

"Do not suppose that I have come to bring peace to the earth. I did not come to bring peace, but a sword. For I have come to turn a man against his father, a daughter against her mother, a daughter-in-law against her mother-in-law- a man's enemies will be the members of his own household."

Matthew 10:34-36 ®NIV

Unfortunately, my circumstances are not necessarily unique. Divorce made my sister, mom and I very close. We were an emotionally enmeshed threesome. We stood up for each other, we laughed and cried together and often the lines of authority were blurred. My mom needed a friend and a partner in parenting, I became both.

In all honesty, I do not have many memories specifically of my mom prior to the divorce. Although I believe that my parents loved one another, violence, alcohol, drugs, alleged infidelity and the stress of life just got the best of their marriage. These negative things dominate most of my childhood memories.

I do recall a few things about my mom pre-divorce. She was beautiful. She had big hazel eyes, with long eye lashes that curled up and cast a shadow mid cheek. Her smile was big, bright and straight. Her course, full bodied hair was always stylish. My mom stood at 5'1", weighing about 100 pounds with curves. Everyone noticed her when she walked into a room.

My mom could sing and play the guitar like Loretta Lynn, Tammy Wynette and Ann Murray all rolled up into one. Her voice was full. It gave me a warm feeling all over. She sang in the shower, in the car, while cooking, it seemed she always sang. But it was a special treat when she pulled out her guitar. We would get a private concert. My sister and I would dance and sing with her. My dad would look at her as if he was falling in love for the first time.

Mom also baked and cooked wonderfully. She would let me crack the eggs and hold the electric mixer. Afterwards we would lick the beaters and the bowl. Then she would push a kitchen chair up to the sink and let me do the dishes. I felt like such a big girl, now I praise God for a dishwasher and kids to unload it!

The most powerful memory I have is her touch when I fell ill. While quietly humming a pretty tune she'd brush my cheek tucking my hair behind my ear. She smelled lightly of perfume, coffee and cigarettes. Comforting smells, my mom's smell.

My memories of her are clearer after the divorce and, of course, the older I got. When the divorce was nearly final, we moved from the town we grew up in and away from our dad. This move was to be a secret between us girls. She asked me to promise not to tell my dad we were leaving. I spent Christmas with him that year, knowing we were leaving the next day and might never see him again. But I felt responsible to protect my mom. I felt sick to my stomach when I left my dad. My sister and I didn't see him for over a year. Thereafter we only saw him during the summer, but not every summer. I did not spend another Christmas with him until my thirties.

One summer, I chose to go to my dad's house. As I packed my mom came into my room to express her anger and disappointment in me for going she said, "It feels like you are splitting my guts open and pissing on them."

She worked relentlessly on me that day trying to get me

to stay. I went anyhow. When I returned, she informed me she had cleaned out my room while I was gone. She presented this information as if she had done something nice for me, like a welcome home gift. However, she had torn down all of my posters and thrown things away she said were "clutter". I cried for hours.

I continued to go and see my dad every opportunity I could, not because it made her mad and not because he deserved it, but because he is my dad. Still, she had a hard time accepting my choice. She took it personally. For a long time my parents seemed primarily focused on hurting one another through us. We were more like pawns in a game of retaliation; we were the rope in a vicious game of tug-a-war.

A clean house was extremely important to my mom. The roaring sound of a vacuum sucking its way through my bedroom woke me every Saturday morning. Mom dedicated Saturday to cleaning. She taught me how to clean the bathtub. I would put on rubber gloves and scrub.

Upon completion, with a scrutinizing look on her face, she would run her hand throughout the tub. If she could feel any rough spot, she required I wash the entire tub over. There was a particular way to do everything. Towels tri-folded, dishes towel dried, clothes washed in cold, and all counters wiped down spotless, "a place for everything and everything in its place."

Which actually sounds a little more like Mary Poppins than my mom; she said something more like, "put your shit away before I throw it away."

I'd tense up after school as it got closer to her coming home. Walking around the house making sure everything was in its place and the dishes were done.

My mom's moods were fairly unpredictable. We tippy toed around until we knew what mood she was in. She had a fierce temper and I tried very hard not to set it off. She would cuss like a sailor, the F word being one of her favorites. When angry she yelled relentlessly until I had forgotten what made her mad. Her famous motto, "If you make your bed you'd better be ready to lay in it!

Mom did not have a lot of luck with men, but that did not stop her from trying. She married four times and had many boyfriends. She seemed generally critical of men with expectations that set them up for failure. She made remarks about how stupid men are, but truly seemed to determine her own self worth by how a man treated her. My mom perfected the art of flirting. Old or young, she could turn a man's head. I found it fascinating how she seemed to be in the middle of a stretching routine when a man was around. She could at any given moment drop to the floor to show her impressive flexibility. In retrospect it was odd, but she seemed to make it appear perfectly normal.

My mom, just like everyone, simply wanted to find love. I will forever be convinced she was most heart broken when she divorced her second husband, who was also her third. He was unfaithful during both marriages. She tried to love him and support him while he attempted to fulfill his dreams, but he was out of work and mostly unmotivated. I do not know if I have ever seen her more devastated than when they finally split.

She was all over the emotional map; she lost weight, started drinking and taking prescription medications for depression and anxiety.

I had moved out of the house to go to college, but moved back in with her after she had a particularly bad night. I was out with friends when I got a call from my Aunt Maxine. She had stopped by to see my mom and found her drunk and crying. She had her gun out and was talking in circles about my step dad and the pain she was in. She repeatedly stated she wanted to kill him.

While my mom was in the bathroom my aunt took the gun and placed it in her car. She was genuinely concerned about how my mom would respond once she noticed the missing gun. So, she called me and asked me to come over and help. When I got there, my mom had not yet noticed that my aunt had taken her gun. She seemed to find it a little amusing that I had been called. She was apologetic, tearful and tired. She eventually surrendered to sleep and I tucked her in bed, assuring her I would stay the night.

A few days later, I moved back in with her. One evening we talked about her marriage and I asked, "Are you mourning the loss of this man or the loss of who you thought this man could have been?" It was as if a light came on. We had a good time that night.

She asked me how I had gotten to be so wise and with a cocky college smile I acknowledged the impressiveness of my insight. After that night, things seemed to improve for her a bit. She still drank, but it seemed minimal. I did not see evidence that she continued to use prescriptions. She took up new hobbies and was always busy doing something or going somewhere.

However, her continued advice to me about men remained, "Make sure you get an education and can take care of yourself, because eventually all men leave."

I understood why she said this, but refused to take it to heart. I wanted to be a part of a beautiful love story one day. I was a hopeless romantic when it came to love. I still am.

Mom liked to talk with us about everything. There was no subject off limits. She talked with us about sex just as easily as she did about homework. She was tough, but I felt comfortable telling her nearly anything. Many of my friends felt the same way. She was fiercely protective and stood up for us. Once a teacher told me to eat everything on my lunch tray, but I refused.

I told the teacher I would throw up if I ate the cold slaw with peanuts and raisins. Her well intentioned philosophy; everything on the lunch tray had to be eaten unless you had an allergy. She made me eat it and I threw up. I went home and told my mom. She contacted my teacher and told her, "From now on, Leslie is allergic to anything she does not want to eat."

It felt great seeing my teacher the next day, knowing my mom had stood up for me. She never failed to make me feel like she would try to protect me if she could.

As for believing in God, my mom had a fairly vague and boxed idea of God. I was on the phone one evening in high school with a close male friend. He told me about the end of the world. He told me about Christ, how He will one day judge each of us. This disturbed me and when we hung-up I began to cry. My mom came into the room and asked what was wrong. I told her about what I had learned. She responded, "Well, I would not want to have a God that judged me. I think that God is happy if I am happy. Don't take that stuff too literally."

I look back on that brief lesson on Theology and think she was half right, God is happy when I'm happy and I believe He morns when I morn. However, we will all one-day stand before Him to be judged. I do take this literally. I do not believe we can create God to be what we want Him to be. He created us. We cannot take Him out of the box when we need Him. He is constant and knowing. We cannot rationalize His rules according to what we have learned here on earth. If this were so why believe at all? What kind of power does a God who we create have? These truths I now know, but before, I too had a designer God in a box.

It was not easy on my mom when I got married. It was especially difficult for her when my husband and I had kids. Some of what my mom taught me, I ended up disagreeing with in my role as a parent. However, some of it stuck. For instance, she taught me to stand up for what I believe, but I think she always thought I would believe the same way she did.

As I told you earlier, it was a little over a year into marriage when I began taking God and His word literally. I would not know it for a while, but the day the Lord took the blinders off my eyes was the day a sliver embedded itself in my mom and I's relationship. It was one that would fester for years until fully infected.

There was a transformation inside of me. God was pruning. This was often uncomfortable as I realized I was not the person he called me to be. I became more conservative in my thinking and remorseful about my past behaviors. The light shined on things in my world and created a gap of darkness between my mom and me.

She thought I had gone overboard and she developed resentment towards Pat. No matter how I tried to explain my relationship with God, she wanted to blame Pat. We had a few relationship-eroding episodes that ultimately were about my sticking to what I believe and her feeling judged by what I believe.

As I mentioned earlier, my mom had several boyfriends. She liked bringing them over and introducing them to us. She was an affectionate person and would hold hands, kiss and hug her dates. At one time, she had been dating a man named Jim for several months and had brought him to our house frequently. We liked him very much and the kids had begun asking if he would be their new grandpa. One Saturday we were preparing for Emily's birthday party. My mom called and asked if she could bring Bill to Emily's party. I asked who Bill was and she told me that he was a man she had been seeing. I asked about Jim and she advised me they broke up.

I said, "Mom, maybe we could meet Bill another day. Today is not the day to bring him over. Emily and Sam are pretty attached to Jim and they will be sad to hear you have broken up. Maybe if you and Bill continue to date and it becomes serious we could meet him."

"You are a self righteous holier than thou bitch. You just do not want to see me happy!"

I tried to explain to her that it was Emily's birthday and I did not want her to be sad. I wanted her to understand that although her happiness was very important to me my priority was my kids. She wanted to know how bringing a new boyfriend to the party would be bad for the kids.

I explained, "When you bring someone over you hug, kiss and hold hands with them. In our house, those actions mean something, so it is confusing to the kids. I want them to believe that love can last and that intimate actions are for the person you love. I also do not want them to become accustomed to attaching to people and then letting them go."

"You are unrealistic and eventually you will cause your kids to hate you for teaching them idealistic views and not about the real world."

"It's true, I would rather the kids know more about what is not of this world than what is of this real world."

After two hours of her yelling at me, the phone call ended. My stomach in knots, I turned to my Bible. I said a short prayer and opened the book randomly, "Do not suppose that I have come to bring peace to the earth. I did not come to bring peace, but a sword. For I have come to turn a man against his father, a daughter against her mother, a daughter-in-law against her mother-in-law – a man's enemies will be the members of his own household." Matthew 10:34-36

I found comfort in those words. I didn't suddenly feel good about the exchange with my mom. The comfort came in knowing God knows things like this will happen between people.

5

BOUNDARIES

"Train a child in the way he should go, and when he is old he will not turn from it."

Proverbs 22:6 ®NIV

Establishing boundaries with my mom whittled away at our relationship. I have no regrets. I love my mom and forever will. She taught me to stand up for what I believe and although she did not like that I used those tools on her. I believe part of her understood I was looking after my family and what I thought was best for my kids. I think partially she was hurt because she knew I was right.

There were times she would tell me I was a good mom or share her regrets as a mom. I always told her I thought she did a great job, the best she could with her circumstances.

It sounds weird but I think in a way my life, marriage and the way we raise our kids was something she envied and that made her angry. The way I lived my life made her feel judged.

Maybe I was being too hard on my mom and I totally understand why she felt judged. However, here is why; my parents have been married ten times between the two of them. With ten marriages come different sets of grandparents, stepsiblings and extended family relationships. Not to mention the countless individuals they dated in-between the marriages. It was hard to accept the loss of people in my life. I do not believe it should be that way and I want my kids to believe love can stay. To me it was and is a subject worth standing my ground on. Love that stays is the foundation in which my husband and I build our family and we dream it will effect generations to come.

6

AGREE TO DISAGREE

"Be on your guard; stand firm in the faith; be men of courage; be strong. Do everything in love."

Corinthians 16:13-14 ®NIV

Eventually my mom and I found some peace or an understanding in our relationship. I was the "Jesus Freak" and we were not ever 100% comfortable around one another, but we found a way to enjoy each other. I had seen some changes in my mom over the last 5 years of her life. Mom increased her alcohol intake significantly. She began to once again take medications for anxiety and depression. She did not stay with any one doctor for very long and often self dosed her medications. She would mix her medicines with alcohol. Her physical health also declined. She gained quite a bit of weight and began smoking again 20 years after she quit. She had difficulty keeping a job and changed residences frequently.

I have my theory as to why she started some self-destructive behavior. I think her world just got too quiet. There was really nothing else to survive. She had a horrific childhood.

I know she was emotionally and physically abused. Her family was poor and uneducated. She was the first in her family history to graduate high school and go on to college. My mom set high standards for her life and pushed through with a vengeance. She was very critical of herself and life simply gave her too much down time to dwell on regret and failures. In addition, I think she felt shame about secrets she carried.

When a person's constant chaotic world no longer presents with chaos, what else is there to survive other than thoughts buried deep inside?

7

LAST VISIT

"Praise be to the God and Father of our Lord Jesus Christ, the Father of compassion and the God of all comfort, who comforts us in all our trouble, so that we can comfort those in any trouble with the comfort we ourselves have received from God."

2 Corinthians 1:3 ® NIV

My mom made an unexpected visit to our house one week before her death. Pat and I were on a walk when she arrived. I was surprised as I approached the house and saw her car. She was sitting with our daughter looking at photo albums. I could tell she wasn't doing well just by the expression on her face. She looked like a bully waiting to pick a fight. Her words slurred; her mouth was dry and smelled of alcohol. She put the photo albums down and the three of us sat and visited for a few minutes. While we were talking, my daughter asked, "Mom can I go to Samantha's house tonight?"

"Nope, not tonight girly, you have too much to do around here."

To which my mom made one of those huff sounds and shook her head, like a teenager saying, "whatever." I ignored this and changed the subject, asking her how her job was going.

Before she could answer my husband walked in the room, put his hand on her shoulder and said, "Hi. It's nice to see you. Where's Bill?"

Like a hot poker scorched her she flinched and said, "Bill's at a conference and I'm gonna play."

"Well enjoy. I'm going to go outside and get some things done."

I could tell mom had made Pat uncomfortable. She made me uncomfortable. I knew he figured it was best to leave her alone.

A few minutes after Pat left mom announced she too

was leaving. With a cocky smile she added,

"I'm outta here. I'm going to your sister's. I'm gonna have some fun. I'm going to sleep alone and have some drinks. No one is going to tell me what I can and can't do."

Then she looked at my daughter and said, "I'm so sorry you gotta have her as a mom. Don't worry it won't be forever."

I forced a smiled and tried to make light of it. I put my arm around Emily and said, "Yup, poor you stuck with me for a little while longer."

Emily put her arm around me and smiled. My mom walked backwards down the walkway loudly exclaiming she was going to go and have some fun. I waved at her and told her to have a nice time.

When she left I went into my bedroom and cried, kicking and hitting the bed. Pat came in, "Hey, are you ok?"

"No, I'm not. She rips me up inside. Sometimes I wish she was dead!"

After my tantrum, I called my sister feeling she deserved a fair warning about mom's mood. My sister thanked me and said she would be hiding all of her alcohol.

I told her to call if she needed anything. Apparently, they had a nice time together, besides a few extended naps, mom was good company.

8

THE LAST STRAW

"Instead, speaking the truth in love, we will in all things grow up into him who is the Head, that is, Christ."

Ephesians 4:15 ®NIV

Later that week I got a call from my step dad, Bill. Yes, she married him. He asked, "Have you heard from your mom today."

"No. Why?"

"Well, she was scheduled to come to my office today to decorate for Christmas. She never showed up. I've gone to the house. I've driven the routes she would have taken and I've been calling her cell phone all day. There is no sign of her. At the house everything is in order, but there was a broken glass on the kitchen floor."

"Well, I hate to say it, but have you checked the police station?"

"I called, but there have been no accidents today."

"No, I mean have you called to see if she has been arrested?"

"Arrested? Why would she have been arrested?"

"Bill, maybe she has been arrested for drunk driving. She has been drinking in the morning, sometimes wine and sometimes vodka in her coffee. Did you not know this?"

"No, I did not know this. I mean I know she drinks a lot some times, but I did not know she had been drinking in the morning. I'll call the police and call you back if I find anything out."

I knew in my gut mom had been arrested. My sister, Kristen was in complete panic, with visions of mom's car upside down in the river. Kristen waited anxiously for the news of my mom's where–a-bouts. I on the other hand, waited with dreaded anticipation, knowing we would soon be dealing with something ugly.

The phone rang, "Leslie, its Bill. You are right. She has been arrested. I'm going to go and get her now."

"Why would you do that? Let her stay there. She could use a little of her own medicine right now. She made this bed and she needs to lay in it! She would never come to get you or me for that matter!"

"I'm going."

Bill hung up. I sat there for a few minutes feeling badly for how I spoke to him. I called back and left a voice mail, "Bill, I'm sorry for the way I spoke to you. I know you are worried and trying to do the right thing. Please call when mom gets home. I want to know she is safe."

Stomach acid built up and my nerves were wired as I waited for Bill to call. Like a coach on the side lines I encouraged myself, *you can do it! Tell her the truth in love. Don't let her deny the drinking. Let her know you love her but be honest. You can't help if you ignore the problem.*

Finally the phone rang, "It's Bill, we are home."

"How is she?"

"She's exhausted and upset. Do you want to talk with her?"

"If she doesn't mind, I would."

Initially, I heard faint breathing, then this flat lifeless voice, "Hello."

"Hey mom, are you ok?"

"I'm fine, but I'm gonna fight this. I've already started looking up lawyers. You wouldn't believe how they treated me. They won't find anything in my system."

"Mom, I love you very much. I know you've been through a hard time (Deep breath), but I don't believe you. We know about the vodka in the coffee and sometimes the wine. You have been drinking a lot and mixing it with medications. No matter what though, we will help you get through this."

Tension hung heavy between my mom and I then she broke the silence with her flat voice, "You are wrong. I don't care what you think. I'll have a lawyer."

Gently I responded, "If I'm wrong, I'm so sorry. I do not want to hurt you. How about you get some rest and we'll talk again tomorrow?"

"That's Fine." Then she hung up the phone.

9

YOUR VOICE

"I pray that out of his glorious riches he may strengthen you with power through his Spirit in your inner being, so that Christ may dwell in your hearts through faith. And I pray that you, being rooted and established in love, may have power, together with all the saints, to grasp how wide and long and high and deep is the love of Christ, and to know this love that surpasses knowledge- that you may be filled to the measures of all the fullness of God."

Ephesians 3:17-19 ®NIV

I waited all day to hear from mom. I didn't want to call knowing I had made her angry. It seemed best to let her contact me. While doing laundry in the early evening, the phone rang. I answered the phone and heard a familiar voice that locked my spine and sent chills over my body. It was mom, but with a voice I can only describe as demonic. I have experienced this voice coming from her a few other times. This voice was icy cold, angry and full of hate.

She seethed "I want to talk to you! I am so sick of you judging me and everyone except for the people whose ass you have your lips attached to!"

When I first heard her voice I knew it was going to be a terrible, likely abusive tongue-lashing. Having experienced it before in recent years, I knew to brace myself because it would be like getting into a boxing ring with the devil.

However, I had resolved myself to hearing her out, but that is all my mom was able to say to me before I hung up the phone.

It was not a decision. My finger simply moved to the "off" button and that was that.

Shocked, I pulled the phone away, stared at my finger on the off button, *Oh man that is really going to tick her off!*

I figured after hanging up on her it would not be a good idea to pick up if she called back. I told my kids to let the phone ring if anyone called. Only a few minutes passed before the phone did ring again.

She left a message in the same seething voice, "Feels good, doesn't it!"

Those were her last words to me. I knew my mom was not well. Tormented by evil is how she sounded. I immediately called my friend Teri. Teri and I prayed for her. We prayed for protection over her.

The first reaction I get from everyone who hears about my last encounters with my mom is to console me for the guilt I must feel. Well, there has been a ton of guilt. I shake my head in disbelief I actually said the words, I wish she were dead. In my heart, I did not mean those words. I knew at the time and I still know, it was an off the cuff response to being hurt. Still the irony slaps me in the face.

As for our last phone call, I truly had resolved myself to hearing her out even knowing she was going to say terrible things to me. I took a deep breath and prepared to listen. I surprised myself when I hung up. I have agonized over that moment. I have wondered if I would have stayed on the phone, could our conversation have made a difference in her choice. I have resolved myself to never knowing the answer. However, I do not think I alone pushed the off button. I believe God gave me a nudge.

He knew what my mom was going to do and what her last words to me would be. I believe His love is vast and deep for us. Her final words to me could have been so much worse if I had stayed on the phone.

I believe He does protect us. I know He was with my

mom when she made her choice and he protected her in ways I cannot begin to understand. We are not to lean on our own understanding and so I try not to. There is freedom in this.

We have no idea what happens between God and another person before they take their last breath.

Diary entry; *"May the God of hope fill you with all joy and peace as you trust in him, so that you may overflow with hope by the power of the Holy Spirit" (Romans 15:13 NIV) This is what I opened my Bible to as I was seeking some comfort days before the 2 year anniversary of my mom's suicide. It was like being able to sit down and have a brief comforting conversation with God. Then it struck me, it is Him, His living breathing words speaking to me. It is not an accident that I should stumble upon words like this at a time such as this. He is here with me. This does not mean that my outlook on life is always full of sunshine and roses. There are times like today I still feel profound sadness and just want, need to feel it. I'm going to soak up the sadness today…bathe in it.*

10

GRIEF THE UNINVITED GUEST

"O Lord, hear my prayer, listen to my cry for mercy; in your faithfulness and righteousness come to my relief."
Psalm 143:1 ®NIV

Grieving can make you feel crazy. I felt like a piece of fragile glass thrown against a wall. Fragments of who I am were spread all over the place. I would try desperately to pick up the pieces, but they were everywhere and some of them were much too small to ever be retrieved.

There have been times when I was laying in bed on my side with my hands curled up under my chin wondering if this is how my stepdad found her. I have put a pillow over my head, put my fingers in the shape of a gun like a little boy might do while playing cops and robbers. I've put that "gun" to the pillow and shot, trying to come to grip with the final moments of mom's life.

Morbid thoughts come to life. I have been tempted numerous times to read the police report. I've wanted to call the arresting officers. We (my sister, step dad and me) even went so far as to hire a lawyer to find out if the officers could be at fault for my mom's choice. The vague note my mom left, blaming the officers in the jail for her decision, prompted this.

Ultimately, the lawyers did not find anything that would make a case, but they did try. I thank them for their sensitivity and the effort they put into the case. Every moment I have spent giving energy to the situation has left me feeling so defeated. The more details I knew about her death the more burdened I felt. I would sense God saying, "No no, don't look there, look here. My grace is sufficient" and my hope would once again grow in meager doses.

Still, grief is a strange thing. It's like your life is a record with a scratch in it. It's stuck on one spot, skipping back replaying the one line over and over again. It's like being in a sci-fi movie. You are not functioning in the same space and time as the rest of the world. The experience is vast, unpredictable, personal and yet universal. There are five text book stages to grief; denial, anger, bargaining, depression and acceptance. I trudged through every single stage, revisiting each several times over. The words are not elaborate enough for how I felt when in the throes of each. I felt broken.

Shock came before denial. Like I had been in a traumatic car accident, my body felt cold and shaky. My body trembled; my mouth could not form words. It took weeks to regain the strength to get through a day without feeling exhausted. My mind had difficulty taking it in. It's like a computer trying to down load a file, but the memory was full. I would try to take it in repeatedly. I'd shake my head, blink my eyes, and begin trying to process the information again.

My body hurt all over. I could feel my heartache and my emotions were spinning around like a nail in a dryer. My stomach and head hurt. The pain was penetrating.

My muscles were knotted up. At times, I wanted to rip my skin off and escape. I recall driving on the highway days after her death and it actually crossed my mind to veer off the road. Running my car over a cliff or hitting a pole sounded a little bit inviting. I entertained the idea for a few minutes, *at 60 mph it could all be over in seconds.* It surprised me I would have such a thought particularly in light of why I was in so much pain, but that's how excruciating it felt. My mind was erased of love. I didn't think about my kids or husband. I didn't think about what the action would mean in the long run, the pain consumed me. That brief window into what my mom must have felt frightened me.

I was in a state of bewilderment. Confused initially by the news, it's just not information one can easily wrap their mind around. Then waking up each day and deciding what to wear was confusing. Making simple decisions; should I eat, should I get dressed, those decisions were strenuous to make.

I took a week off from work. I had been back only a few days when my good friend Teri, who I mentioned earlier, advised me I had moved a pen from one spot and back to the other hundreds of times. She then took me by the arm and said, "Go home. You need more time and that pen will still be here looking for its rightful place when you return."

I smiled, then cried and went home.

I felt denial about how my mom died. It is hard enough to cope with the loss of a parent. It was how she died that knocked the wind out of me. I kept reaching for some other solution. I even said to my husband, "She was not the type to kill herself. She was more the type you wanted to kill. Maybe Bill killed her."

I could understand her husband being angry with the DUI and tired of my mom. I could see him reaching a boiling point and not wanting to deal with unpredictable moods, her substance abuse and her legal problems. Maybe too many episodes of CSI made her murder easier to stomach than her suicide.

Perhaps murder was easier to accept than suicide because it would relieve me of the weighted guilt I felt. Guilt would overwhelm me and I would surrender to it, curl myself up in a ball and wail, "I'm so sorry I failed you! I was a terrible daughter. I did judge you. You hated me and I deserved it. I should have answered the phone. I should not have told you I didn't believe you. I should have seen the signs!" I was a prizefighter kicking my own butt. Guilt sucked the life out of me.

I was also acutely aware of feeling ashamed. The moment came when Pat asked what I wanted him to tell people from work. We work in the same office and he was calling my supervisor to let him know I would not be into work for a while. I told him to tell the truth. I tend to feel that way about most things that make us feel embarrassed or ashamed. Tell the ugly truth. We all have one to tell. So Pat told the truth. Logically I know what I just wrote about the truth to be, true. Still there was shame. What would people think of me having a mother who committed suicide?

Will they think I come from a crazy family? Who am I now? My persona, my reputation……the person I want people to think I am will it all be questioned? I even found myself feeling ashamed for looking like my mom. I have her mannerisms. I walk like her. I laugh like her. I have the same facial expressions when annoyed. I have the same head bob when I'm mad. I would find myself consciously trying to walk differently. I would catch my reflection in the mirror and feel nauseated. I apologized to my sister several times when I could read her thoughts, *you looked just like mom.* I hated knowing my very presence reminded her of mom.

Anger was a huge part of my grief. Anger seems to be the emotion that has stuck with me the longest. In fact, I feel peace knowing I may always feel angry with my mom. I have concluded this is ok. As long as the anger does not dominate my love for her and as long as it does not consume me, it seems to be a healthy response to her act. I feel angry with her when something wonderful happens with her grandchildren and she isn't here to see it. I feel most angry with her when my children or my sister struggle with sorrow because of her.

I want to scream at her, "They do not deserve this pain!" When my kids cry because of my mom's choice, I cannot help but to label suicide as one of the most selfish acts and anger stings me.

I'm stunned by how far the tentacles of suicide stretch. I was having lunch with Teri recently and we talked about my mom. Teri's chin started to quiver and she said, "I don't think I've ever told you this, but I still struggle with some guilt about your mom's death. You had to develop a lot of boundaries with her and I encouraged you. I even prayed with you to have strength to stand your ground with her. I sometimes wonder if things would have turned out differently if I hadn't done that."

Five years later my friend was still carrying this burden. That makes me mad at my mom. I replied, "Oh friend, I'm so sorry you have been carrying that around. This is what I know to be true, God knew from the beginning of my mom's life how her life would end. He gave me the gift of beautiful, strong and faithful friends to help me navigate my way through this storm. You have been at the helm. This event has been colossal and nearly destroyed me. Had I not had boundaries the wounds would have been deeper. You did exactly what God calls us to do for one another and I'm so thankful."

Suicide is a shadow in my home. I pray light over it all of the time, but it is there waiting to trip someone. It affects my kids in profoundly deep ways. Anger is not a harsh enough word for how I feel about that.

The hardest thing to fight is depression. There is an opportunity for the circumstance to consume me every day. I have felt like darkness is crushing me. It all lunges for me. I feel like the descriptive words of grief are alive, hanging on me. It takes every bit of energy to look to God. Truthfully, some days I simply do not want to. I want to feel despair and avoid God. During these times, there is always the faint knowing that I can't stay this way.

It starts to feel uncomfortable. It gnaws at me and before I know it, life becomes about me, my despair. I am convinced times like this will lead to eventual loss of hope. Then I decide I can't go on like this, ignoring my blessings, forgetting the one who suffered far greater pain than I. I make a conscious effort to think on my blessings to pull me through the day.

I did not necessarily find myself bargaining in the traditional way. I did not try to ask God to bring my mom back to life or to somehow make it all untrue and in return I would be a better Christian. However, I did ask God for reassurance.

Both of our kids needed reassurance their grandma made it to heaven. Of course I reinforced their hope. The truth is I had the same question. While in prayer I told God how afraid I was that He did not have my mom. I prayed for Him to have her. I prayed that she felt abundantly loved resting in his arms. I pictured her as innocent child being cared for by a loving, patient and kind Father. I desperately want my images of her to be real. I want to see all the stains of this ugly world washed from her.

A few weeks after her passing I took a walk and talked with God, "God please let me know you have her. Let me know by sending me a sign. Maybe you could send me a moose."

A moose? Sure why not. I have never had a desire to see a moose. I've lived in the Northwest my whole life and haven't had a hankering to track a moose. I have no idea why I asked for a moose, but I did. After all, others before me have asked for more outlandish things. Moses asked to see His glory. Surely he wouldn't mind sending me a moose.

For seven months I looked for a moose everywhere; driving to work, going to the store, picnicking in the park My sister and I took a trip to Montana and I thought, *my odds must be better in Montana. They probably have tons of moose.* Ten hours there and ten hours back with my face plastered to the window, no moose.

One morning I got up a little early to have some prayer time. With Pat out of town I had decided to go to work late so I could see the kids off to school. I had not spent any quality time in prayer for weeks. Most of my prayers were completed while stuck in traffic. So, this morning as I prayed I asked God to remind me He is with me. It felt good to take the time to be with Him. My prayer time ended when Emily came up the stairs to eat breakfast. We had a short visit and I told her Sam had crawled into my bed earlier in the morning so I was going to go and wake him up. Emily offered to go with me.

We walked into my room and I leaned over to give Sam a kiss as Emily opened the curtains. Suddenly Emily shouted, "Oh my gosh, there is a moose in the yard!" I shot straight up and ran to the window.

I have terrible eyesight and immediately asked Emily to help me find my glasses or to get the binoculars. I smashed myself to the window like a kid ogling a toy store window while the large brown blob meandered through the field. Emily handed me the binoculars. I could hardly believe it. Was I hysterical? Yes, I was totally hysterical. I was bawling and praising God.

At one point, my son put his hand on my shoulder and said, "Mom, are you all right? It's just a moose."

I sighed, "Oh no guys, that's a love letter from God."

Up until that moment, I had not told anyone about my child like prayer. I told my kids and with big grins on their faces they both said, "That is so cool!"

I didn't think to take a picture of the moose until the brown blob disappeared into the trees. That's ok though, I can still see it perfectly.

Some might say it's a coincidence. It's not. I've lived 40+ years in Montana and Washington State. I've been to Idaho 100's of times; I've never seen a moose before. The moose's stroll through my yard took all of 30 seconds. If one thing would have been different about my morning I would have missed the moose.

God timed it beautifully. Pat went out of town so I went to work late to help the kids get ready for school. Sam had climbed into bed with me. My conversation with Emily ended at the right time. She opened the curtains and the love letter was delivered.

11

ACCEPTANCE, IT'S JUST AN EARTH SUIT

"Even though I walk through the valley of the shadow of death, I will fear no evil, for you are with me; your rod and your staff, they comfort me."

Psalm 23:4 ®NIV

I had been given a small amount of my mom's ashes from my step dad. Soon after receiving them I felt an urge to release them. I struggled with having this little urn. I did not want it around. I remembered my mom telling me when she died to spread her ashes somewhere I like to go and then have a party.

I could not party, but spreading her ashes I could do and wanted to do. There is an old cemetery placed amongst the wheat fields by my house. I can picture farmers from a 100 years ago laying their loved ones to rest here. I imagine families gathering to comfort the local from this small town. I find it peaceful. I'm fascinated by the headstones and the history. I chose to spread my mom's ashes there.

The arctic air whipped my hair across my face. The brilliance of the sun lit up the fields, I could feel snow sneaking around the corner. Pat, the kids and I drove to the cemetery. I picked a spot beneath a weathered lilac tree and dug a small hole. The stubborn ground made shoveling difficult. Pat fought with the urn until he cut himself before opening it. My family prayed while I released the ashes into the air. They blew perfectly toward the fields as small fragments of bone fell to the ground. I buried the urn under the lilac tree and cried. After we got home, my son asked me to take him back to the cemetery so he could play my mom a song on the trumpet. Just he and I went back and he played. The sun sat like an orange ball of flames on the horizon as an owl took off over our heads.

ACCEPTANCE, IT'S JUST AN EARTH SUIT

It was a beautiful moment. I think my mom would have liked that little "party", it was the best I could do.

Days later I walked back to the cemetery alone. I felt compelled to take care of something. I needed to collect as many pieces of the bone I could and place them under the tree.

I don't know why I wanted to do this, but I wanted to. Afraid and with hesitant hands I began picking up the pieces from the dirt.

The fear drifted from me and I smiled through tears. There was something comforting about collecting and caring for these pieces. I became certain; our bodies are nothing more than a house for our spirit, just sheetrock and 2x4's. My mom was not there, it was just a house she wanted to move out of. It was strange and comforting. Peace and acceptance washed over me.

12

UNIVERSAL, YET UNIQUE

"Not only so, but we also rejoice in our sufferings, because we know that suffering produces perseverance; perseverance, character; and character, hope. And hope does not disappoint us, because God has poured out his love into our hearts by the Holy Spirit, whom he has given us."

Romans 5:3-5 ®NIV

Grief is something we cannot avoid. We will all experience it. It is universal, but very personal and unique. Although my sister and I had both lost our mom, we grieved differently. We could relate to one another, to the pain. However, we had our own way of dealing with it. We had to find a way to accept and respect the way the other grieved.

Kristen wanted to know everything. She wanted details of mom's death, police reports and the pictures. She found out mom had shot herself in the head, specifically the right temple. She went to the guest room, closed the door, turned on a fan, left a note, laid on her left side, put a pillow over her head and shot. The officers said it was well thought out. She did everything she could to muffle the sound.

I remember when my sister told me these details. It felt like my blood froze. I choked out, "Stop! I can't have this information. I can't store this stuff. If you find out any more about mom's death, I don't want you to share it with me."

I feared what was left of my mind would surely crumble with more information. No detail would help me climb out of the deep pit. I knew I needed to get out. I had to grasp hold of anything good I could.

My sister told me she was thinking about getting pictures of the crime scene. I pled with her not to get the pictures. The mind is not meant to have images of one's mother shot in the head.

I'm so thankful she did not get them. When it came time to gather mom's belongings, Kristen wanted everything. She told my step dad she wanted the mattress my mom died on, which he did not give her. She seemed desperate to grasp any little thing about mom she could. She collected hair from her hair brushes, wore her bras and filled her home with pictures of her. She fell into a deep depression.

Kristen and I work together. One day she did not show up for work. I called her house several times, but there was no answer. I called her husband and he told me Kristen wasn't doing very well and did not want to go to work. He sounded worried and at a loss for what to do.

I left work early and went to my sister's house. My hands were shaking as I knocked on her front door. Afraid of what I might find, I held my breath until the door opened. Slouched over with a blanket hugging her she whispered, "Hi" and sluggishly walked back to her lazy boy chair. The TV was on mute, the shades were drawn, and the lights out. Her hair hung stringy and unkempt and her clothing looked well worn.

Tearfully I said, "You had me pretty scared. I hesitated to knock on the door because I feared what I might find. What are you doing to yourself, to your family?"

Kristen strained for words, "I don't know. I just feel so sad all of the time. I feel like I'm not supposed to be happy again, like it will hurt her if she sees me happy. I don't want her to think that I've forgotten her."

I thought about what my sister had said and remembered the first time I saw her after she had been told about mom's suicide. I walked into her house and could hear her screaming and retching from her bathroom. I sat on her bathroom floor with her, crying, hugging her and holding back her hair when she threw up. When the tears stopped and the shock took over, I took her hand and said, "Listen to me. We will be ok. We will get through this and we will not let this define us. We will let God and hopes in everything good in our lives define us."

Kristen looked at me through blood shot eyes and said, "I'm afraid. I'm afraid this will define me."

So here we were months later, both dealing with the same loss in two very different ways. Kristen thought I stuffed my pain and said, "I just don't understand why you are where you are with all of this and why I am where I am."

I replied, "I'm not stuffing my pain. Believe me it is relevant every single moment of every single day. I seek counsel, comfort and refuge in God. He has provided me with more strength and better advice than any man can. To make the loss more important than every gain I have in my life is not fair. It's not fair to those I love. To let this tragedy rule my life is not something I am willing to do because despite what has been taken, I have been given so much more. Don't let the evil that surrounded mom's life consume yours. Your children love you and need you. Someday they will have to endure a loss. You have to show them they can make it through. Mom's life ended, not yours. Now, it's time for you to get in the shower. You need to wash. We are throwing mom's bras away and going to lunch and then shopping. You need new bras! I'll buy."

Kristen got up, showered and we went shopping. The bras did get thrown away.

Kristen made a choice. She made a choice every morning after that; why will I get out of bed today? What will define me today?

Most days Kristen found a reason to get up and most days, she was defined by something beautiful and good, like being a mom or a great Social Worker. There were still days when our circumstance creates shadows, but she gets out of bed.

It was important for my sister to allow her feelings to surface, even take over for a while. How she grieved was not any better or worse than the way I did. We both had to learn to live with our loss not in it.

13

A COMMON THREAD

"Be self-controlled and alert. Your enemy the devil prowls around like a roaring lion looking for someone to devour. Resist him, standing firm in the faith, because you know that your brothers throughout the world are undergoing the same kind of sufferings. And the God of all grace, who called you to his eternal glory in Christ, after you have suffered a little while, will himself restore you and make you strong, firm and steadfast. To Him be the power forever and ever, Amen."

Peter 3:10 ®NIV

It has amazed me how people seem drawn to tell me about their own losses since my mom's suicide. It shocked me how many of those losses were from suicide. One man lost his nephew to suicide. Another woman lost both her brother and father to suicide and another woman lost her mother. Yet another woman lost both her parents to suicide.

The stories of loss continued beyond suicide. There was loss of relationships, jobs, health, homes and loved ones through death other than suicide. The list goes on and on. One of the common threads of life is loss. Loss and the process of grieving comes in big and small packages. People grieve the loss of youth, talents, and seasons. Grieving is a part of everyday life. It is an unavoidable process that either evolves or erodes our character, strength and our humanity. It's our choice to ask God for help or to be prideful enough to think we can manage it on our own.

I've pondered how different I once thought I was from most of the people who shared their stories with me. Interestingly, I found that it was only vanity that separated me. I am a prideful person. What I hated most about my loss was feeling broken and weak. When I read Christ's words encouraging me to carry one another's burdens I thought it sounded wonderful. I don't mind at all being strength for someone else. The beauty of those words dulls when you are the one with the burden.

Am I then a tool for those words to be carried out? Did this crazy time in my life allow someone to understand and live the words that Christ taught? I think so. Does it make it easier? I think it does a little. There was no covering this one up. I think I became more real both to others and myself. I truly hated the discomfort I was in. Partially the discomfort came from the loss of my mom and partially it came from the loss of my image. I was a mess for a long time. I had trouble concentrating and this was apparent to my coworkers. I had trouble socializing and this was apparent to my friends. I had trouble organizing and this was apparent to my family. My energy was shot and I looked tired and this was apparent to my acquaintances. Everything that caused me discomfort and made me feel embarrassed for being out of control made certain people, particularly those who had suffered a loss gravitate to me.

We understood each other. A glance from knowing eyes is comforting. I work with a woman whose brother committed suicide a few months after my mom. I had never had a conversation with her only a quick hello by the copy machine. I approached her one day, looked her in the eyes. Like looking in a mirror, she reflected the vacant lost despair I understood all too well. I put my hand on her shoulder and said, "I understand what you are feeling. I just want you to know, you are not alone. My mom took her life a few months ago. If you ever need to talk, I'm here."

A faint light appeared in her eyes and then she cried. We held each other for a few minutes, dusted ourselves off and got back to work. Later that day I received this email, "Leslie, thank you for talking with me. It's comforting knowing that someone else gets it. You threw me a life line."

Diary entry; *I feel like I'm running in circles now. Just when I think I'm done feeling sad, I'm done feeling tired; I'm done feeling angry it all comes back around. I'm sick of feeling like this. God I need you so much. I'd be lost without you. Sorrow have your way with me tonight, but know this! I will walk away eventually stronger, wiser, more mature and over flowing with hope!*

14

THE CHURCH FAMILY

"While Jesus was still talking to the crowd, his mother and brothers stood outside, wanting to speak to him. Someone told him, "Your mother and brothers are standing outside, and want to speak to you."

He replied to him, "Who is my mother, and who are my brothers? Pointing to his disciples, he said, "Here are my mother and my brothers. For whoever does the will of my Father in heaven is my brother and sister and mother." "

Matthew 12: 46-50 ®NIV

Traditionally, the church did exactly what the world designed it to do. We were put on the prayer chain. Our Pastor and Associate Pastor called to offer condolences. Congregation members dropped off food and delivered flowers. The mailbox overflowed with cards. The Associate Pastor put together a meaningful and well thought out sermon for a small memorial gathering. However, after about a week the church disappeared.

Don't get me wrong. I am grateful for all of the help. My family likely wouldn't have eaten for days if it weren't for the members of my congregation. The cards were wonderful and the prayers were desperately needed.

I realize the church is truly called upon to fill in the gaps for Social Services, the government, counselors, families and physicians. They are an over burdened resource so my next suggestion may sound ungrateful and even arrogant. But, I cannot think of a better source to get the job done.

In my experience, the world seems to have a timeline for grieving. In the first week food, calls and cards flood in. Interestingly, in the first week you don't want to eat, can barely utter a word and wouldn't be able to read a card if Rosetta Stone were offering you a million dollars.

By week two, the crisis support disappears. The giant life vacuum sucks them back into their reality, while you hang on for dear life. The one in the midst of loss continues to feel like they are running in jello for months, sometimes years, while the world races by. It is a perfect time for spiritual crisis to fester. Crisis support truly is needed for longer. We need to pace our generosity. Comfort food, supportive company and help around the house should be spread out over the course of weeks, possibly months.

The church family is an important link to giving people hope when they have lost something or someone. Having a person within the church check in with a congregation member throughout the first year of loss could be a vital part of healing. I only know nothing can cause a person to question their faith more than facing loss.

I started thinking even a simple card sent out several different times throughout the first year of grieving could help a person hold on. We are brothers and sisters. We are a family under Christ and should carry one another through a crisis, not deliver a meal and then disappear.

While thinking about this I realized that I have not involved myself enough in my church family. I have not reached out to support members of my family through their crisis. So, I designed a set of five cards. The first card goes out in the first month, when the dust has settled and a person has the where-with-all to pay attention to the words of encouragement. Then cards are sent in the 3rd, 6th, 9th and 12th month. I call the card set, Testify Hope.

I would like every person who has lost a loved one to be reminded that they are not alone, God is with them and a friend is thinking of them.

The simple cards have turned out to be a powerful

gift. Because they come in a post card format there has been an additional blessing that I did not initially think of. I thought that the post card format was convenient. Thus it would not be too difficult for people to remember to put a stamp on a card and drop it in the mail. Not much thought has to go into it. What I didn't think about is how many hands the post card would be in before it got to the recipient.

My friend's mother in law was the first recipient of the cards. She lives in a small rural area and had to go to the local post office to pick up her mail. When she asked the post master for her mail, the woman made this comment, "I hope you don't think I was going through your mail, but I couldn't help but notice the post card. It is beautiful and truly touched me."

I am humbled to know that God gave me this small idea, which is ministering to people in such big ways. I know nothing about this post mistress. I have no idea if she is a believer or not, but a seed was definitely planted. I can't wait till she sees the next 4 cards come through over the course of the year. Who knows what God has planned! I'm just so excited to be a part of it!

Once the cards were designed I contacted my church and asked if I could send these cards out to members of our congregation who experience loss. They embraced this idea. I have sent out several sets. I'd love to see every church adopt a ministry in which those members of the family are contacted through at least the first twelve months of loss. We are called to love one another as Christ loved the church. Being embedded in loss can result in separation from people, church and life in general. It is a perfect time for the enemy to deviously make a person feel completely alone. It's an easy place to be enveloped by darkness and consumed by circumstance. People can get lost in the loss. It is crucial to have a thread to hang onto that pulls them towards faith. The church is that thread. I've discovered that even a small way like a post card could make all the difference.

15

THE MASKS WE WEAR

"Before his downfall a man's heart is proud, but humility comes before honor."

Proverbs 18:12 ®NIV

We should all be perfect or do our darnedest to appear as if we are. When we are not perfect, when we are in the midst of loss the stress of not being perfect is almost as bad to deal with as the circumstances that got us there. After word of my mom's suicide spread I felt vulnerable. I had developed a reputation of being a strong, directed, quick witted, hard working person. In a matter of minutes, I was weak, lost, confused and sluggish. I felt internal pressure to pull myself together and scratch my way back to my reputation.

I've found myself fumbling with my social mask. (Wanting to polish it up and get it back on.) We are an incredibly busy society with little time set aside to deal with our emotions. When you are the one whose mask has fallen off it seems like everyone around you is going about business at superhuman speed. It's impossible to keep up, like chasing your hat in the wind.

Society seems to feel uncomfortable around broken people. So, when we ourselves are broken, we feel like failures. I have spoken with several friends and acquaintances over the past few years that are experiencing some sort of loss. When they show the cracks in their armor and get emotional about what they are going through they all eventually say the same thing, "I'm so sorry for being this way." Universally, they were embarrassed because their mask had fallen off.

One of my dearest friends recently had her mask fall off. Her marriage was unstable. I know divorce was a real consideration for her. For weeks, every time we visited she would end up in tears.

"I feel like a basket case. I have no control. I'm scared, confused and so tired." Within minutes she would frantically wipe her tears away saying, "I'm sorry for being this way." Then try to pull herself together as quickly as possible.

Even my friend Teri who helped me through the loss of my mom apologized to me for crying at work just weeks after her mom passed away.

I asked her, "How are you really doing?"

"I'm fine.... No I'm not! I can't think. I don't know what I'm doing and I'm so embarrassed to be doing this here." Then she said, "I'm sorry for being this way."

This was coming from someone who had not too long before instructed me to extend myself some grace.

Why do we do this to ourselves? Again, there isn't one of us who has not experienced loss. Why do we want to pretend we haven't? Is it vanity?

Every time someone asked me how I was doing I wondered if they really wanted to know.

I make my living as a Social Worker. I'm well practiced at looking people in the eye and helping them through a crisis.

So I thought it was ironic; here I was working in an office full of Social Workers. These are folks born with an extra compassion gene. All of the people I work with are kind and thoughtful people, but I found them passing me by rather quickly. Most asked the rhetorical question, "How are you?" as they dashed on. I started to reply, "I'm fine. I'm Leslie fine Stickel."

It seems there is external and internal pressure to move through grieving quickly. The grieving process is nearly as uncomfortable for those around us as it is for the grieved. Pull yourself together; put on a happy mask and let us all forget about what you have been through. Every one jumps into the emotional community bath, washes off the gunk and hands you a towel.

This is fascinating to me because I believe God's heart yearns for us the most when we are humbled. Going through a loss is humbling. He'd prefer us without our worldly masks, completely vulnerable to being molded by His hands.

16

EVERYTHING IN MODERATION

"Why are you so downcast, O my soul? Why so disturbed within me? Put your hope in God, for I will yet praise him, my savior and my God"

Psalm 42:11 ®NIV

HOPE DEFINED

Many of us would like to move beyond grieving as soon as humanly possible. Unfortunately, it's called a process or stages because it isn't over quickly. When loss has entered our world, which it will, we need to allow ourselves to experience all of it, sometimes revisiting different aspects of grieving multiple times over the course of what can be years. It is however, important to not get stuck in a perpetual state of healing. We cannot indulge grief to the extent that we live in an obsessive realm of self pity.

How do you know when you're stuck? Take cues from your life. For instance, have relationships been affected? Do friends still invite you out or are you alone a lot? Have you had major appetite changes which have lasted longer than the first weeks of the initial shock? Is your sleep restless? Are you drinking more or have you started using drugs? Do you feel tired and is it difficult to "get going" daily?

These can be signs of serious depression. I encourage you first and foremost to contact your church family. They are there to help carry your burden. Prayer is powerful! Encouragement from friends is also powerful. Feeling lonely when dealing with loss is common, but you do not have to be alone. I would also encourage contact with area support groups or individual counseling. You may need to contact your physician about medications.

Like my sister and I, you will have to learn to live with your loss, not in it.

17

FORGO NORMAL

"Let the morning bring me word of your unfailing love, for I have put my trust in you. Show me the way I should go, for to you I lift up my soul."

Psalm 143:8 ®NIV

Part of healing is accepting the finality of the loss (at least here on earth) and to forgo normal. Note I did not suggest you embrace a, "new normal". I don't believe in normal. What exactly is that?

I've never met anyone who is normal. I wasn't "normal" before my mom's suicide. I sure as heck didn't have a chance at it after her suicide. In retrospect, none of my friend's lives are "normal" either. They all experienced some type of difficulty; broken families, alcoholism, death, abuse. There just isn't a perfect life out there.

Truly, the fact that normal does not exist unites us in a way. We do not have anything to be ashamed of when an event impacts our lives. There is always someone who has been there, done that. I say, the grass is always browner on the other side of the fence. We all got our ugly.

In our circumstance it is important to have perspective to know the situation stinks, but we don't. We are not defined by the circumstance. It's also imperative to remember where we are. We are in an imperfect world, where normal does not exist. Perhaps abnormal is the new normal.

Bad things are guaranteed to happen. We have to brace ourselves for the impact and put on the armor of God until Jesus returns! We must move through our circumstances, embrace hope and focus on all that is good in our lives.

My mom and I spent an enjoyable weekend together antique shopping two weeks before she committed suicide. She helped me decide on a hutch I wanted for my living room. We brought it to my house and she helped me fill it. She arranged old books, gathered the perfect knickknacks and even found a way to display an afghan my husband's grandmother made.

The way she placed everything came straight out of a country living magazine. She had a gift for decorating and created what I envisioned.

The first Christmas without my mom came and the kids needed the home to be decorated. I moved the hutch to make room for the Christmas tree and felt a tinge of panic about what to do with it. This space became a small homage to my mom, but I took a deep breath and started.

I rearranged some things and kept other things the way she set them up. I felt some guilt for changing something she left behind. I felt sad to move the last things she touched with loving hands in my home. However, I also felt freedom. Every little thing I moved represented a little freedom from my grief.

There was constant adjustment, there is with any type of loss. Divorce for instance has multiple phases of adjustment. I've seen family and friends devastated by divorce.

Grieving loss of love and thoughts of what the future was supposed to hold. In many instances people lose their home, time with children, money, furniture and even their name.

I know a woman separated from her husband for over a year, who decided to take back her maiden name. The first day with her maiden name came with a great deal of emotions. She spent the evening crying and revisiting her losses.

The feelings confused her and even made her feel a little silly. She tripped over her tongue for months when she said her own name. Soon, the maiden name rolled off her tongue and became easy for her.

People who have lost a job find a new one. Divorced people date and even remarry and the living keep on living.

We come up with new traditions, create new memories, take new pictures, develop hobbies and meet new people. The future family pictures won't have my mom in them, but they will be filled with all the abnormal people I love and will represent new times with them.

18

KIDS

"And he said: I tell you the truth, unless you change and become like little children, you will never enter the kingdom of heaven. Therefore, whoever humbles himself like this child is the greatest in the kingdom of heaven."

Matthew 18: 3-4 ®NIV

Telling our kids their grandma committed suicide was gut-wrenching. Initially, they did not know. Pat and I needed time to gather ourselves. Our kids woke to the sound of my screams that morning. After Pat settled me he went inside to quickly check on them. Unsure of what to tell them and trying to hold everything together he said grandma had died in her sleep and I was very upset. They both shed some tears and they wanted to see me, but Pat asked them to give me a few minutes. Understandingly, they both were content to go downstairs and snuggle up for Saturday morning cartoons.

I went to see the kids an hour or so later. We cried together and they seemed grown up, trying to comfort me. They had questions but I told them I didn't have any answers just yet about grandma's death. The kids both left that afternoon and spent the night with family friends. I needed time and Pat was all about taking care of me.

A few days passed when my daughter, Emily, who is an intuitive child approached me and said, "Mom, I know something more happened to grandma. I don't know what it is and I know you are not ready to tell me, but when you are, I want to know."

Those words from my at the time 12 year old daughter, stirred a peace and an awe inside of me. The Lord paved the way towards what was inevitable and He had already begun preparing Emily.

The following evening Emily came into the kitchen while Pat and I were having one of our hundreds of conversations about why this happened. The conversation stopped when she entered the room and she asked, "Are you ready to tell me what happened to grandma? Did she take too many pills and drink alcohol and then fall asleep?"

With a staggered exhale I said, "Yes honey she did, but she did it on purpose."

"What do you mean? How do you know?"

I then explained that her grandma had committed suicide and she had left a note. I did not have time to think clearly through what to disclose to the kids about how she took her life. I knew I did not want the kids to have images of their grandma shot in the head. The scenario Emily came up with was awful enough.

I can hardly stand the sorrow my heart feels recalling her innocent face, her eyes looked so betrayed as she was coming to grips with what I was telling her. We cried and held each other. We talked a little, but mostly just held on to each other. Emily slept in our room that night and skipped school the next day. We watched a lot of T.V.

Emily's grief, her loss was her own. She went through times when she would not discuss it at all. She is named after my mom, Emily Jean. When I would call her this as I often do, it would make her angry and she would sharply instruct me, "Do not call me that again!"

Emily is a straight A student, but her grades began to decline. I had contacted the principle and told him what our family was dealing with and I know he spoke with her teachers. They were very gracious. I had encouraged Emily several times to talk with someone about everything she was feeling, but she resisted this until one day when she got an F on a test. This was her wake up call.

She finally came to me, "Everything reminds me of grandma. I talk with my friends about her and they try to understand. They say their grandma died too, but their grandma died the way grandmas are supposed to. No one understands!"

Emily began seeing the school counselor and became more open about talking at home. We had a break through conversation one evening when she and I were watching TV together.

"Mom, could you get me some water proof mascara?"

"Why?"

"Sometimes I cry at school about grandma."

I explored the subject a bit more with her and the flood gates opened. Every question I had asked myself about my mom's suicide came out of her sweet innocent mouth. I felt fury towards my mom for taking a piece of my innocent child with her. I ached for my little girl and wanted to scoop her up and rock her like I did when she was a baby.

She asked, "Didn't grandma love me? Didn't she want to see me grow up? Why would she do this?" Emily went on to talk about the weekend prior when my mom stopped by unexpectedly. Emily told me while they were looking at photo albums she sensed grandma wasn't doing well and thought she could smell alcohol on her breath.

Then Emily asked the million dollar question, "Could I have stopped her?"

My baby was carrying such an incredible weight on such young, small and innocent shoulders. My gut twisted when she said this. I decided to tell her about my last few conversations with mom.

I reminded her of how the phone rang the night before her grandma died and how I instructed them to not answer the phone. I shared with her everything my mom said. Emily listened to me intently with large tears gently rolling from her big green eyes (those are my Mom's too). We had this brief look into each other's pain and it was good.

She said, "Oh momma, I hope you don't think it's your fault. I hope you don't think you could have stopped her." The child becoming the parent, she took the words right out of my mouth. I just wanted Emily to understand love or lack of it did not have anything to do with her grandma's decision and what she did was not her fault or mine. Carrying a burden around as monumental as someone taking their own life can crush your spirit and is seemingly impossible for an adult to bear. My poor child was doing this. We wiped away one another's tears, talked and mourned, a peace did settle in us both.

Emily's world gradually settled. Her grades picked back up and she did not seem as preoccupied. She was able to let go to a degree of all of her questions and the burdens she carried.

She is no longer angry when I call her Emily Jean. When we were talking recently she told me that she hopes to have a baby girl some day and she wants to name her Lily. I asked her what the middle name would be, with a peaceful smile on her face she said, "Jean, of course".

With some breaths you can actually feel something leave your body. When she said that I took a deep breath and I released some anxiety and fear.

Sam was different, but I sensed he also knew something. Every other night when I would go to his bed to kiss him good night he would ask a few questions. How his grandma died was in the forefront of his mind.

He would ask, "Did her heart just stop? Did she just close her eyes and take a deep breath (he would then take one) and then just let it out slowly (he would let it out) and that was all?"

Did she do this and he would mimic some dramatic scene he'd seen on TV and finally relax, hanging over his bed with his tongue hanging out. It sounds somewhat humorous, but he was serious. The details of her death were hanging over him. I think there was even some fear about going to sleep, although he did not admit this. About two weeks after her death we decided we needed to tell Sam.

We all gathered in the family room as we often do when we have something to talk about. We told Sam about his grandma's suicide. Sam just looked at me with his big brown eyes and began to cry. His first question, “So, she died on purpose?” The second thing he wanted to know,

“Why?” and then he wanted to know how I knew she killed herself. I told Sam yes she died on purpose and I did not know why. I told him I knew she committed suicide because she left a note. I tried to explain his grandma was very sick and did not know how to deal with her pain and anger.

I was in touch with the school so the teachers, counselor and principles would know our kids were dealing with a unique loss. I followed up with the teachers frequently to make sure they weren’t seeing any red flags we could be missing. I have concern for Sam because it seems he has not processed all this. He is younger, but I think it will come so I try to bring it up with him every now and then. I just watch him closely for signs.

The older he gets the more questions he has. Every now and then, he will have a good cry. He simply says he is thinking about her and what she did.

These days it is fairly rare either of our kids voluntarily bring grandma up. We have yet to start happy reminiscing as we do about Pat’s mom. The kids remember Pat’s mom with nothing but happy thoughts. When they miss her, they think of her. They talk about her funny curly hair, wet kisses and ugly feet. I think right now when the kids miss my mom, they think of the way she died and not about her. My continued hope is time will allow that to fade into the background and they will remember things like her laugh and how short she was.

It is hard enough to manage yourself when you are grieving the loss of something or someone, but I caution you to check in frequently with your kids. They will experience the exact same feelings as you. Contact the school and let the teachers, counselor and principle know what your family is dealing with. I needed all the help I could get.

I also contacted my kid's primary physician. He was supportive and provided me with contact information to a specialist just in case. He also provided me with documentation I needed to take extra time off from work to be with my kids.

Don't be afraid to cry and express anger in front of them. You need to show them it's ok to feel afraid, sad and broken, but you also need to show them they will come out of it and life will be good again. The most important thing for my kids to see me do is to turn to God for strength and to display the hope He has instilled in me. Like me, I know my kids now have a true understanding of what hope is.

19

COUNT YOUR BLESSINGS

"Finally, brothers, whatever is true, whatever is noble, whatever is right, whatever is pure, whatever is lovely, whatever is admirable- if anything is excellent or praiseworthy- think about such things."

Philippians 4:8 ®NIV

Loss can be a permanent wound that grows and festers or it can scar over and serve as a reminder, you made it! Surviving something bad will always ultimately come down to our will and the perspective we want to have. There are a million terrible things I could focus on regarding my mom's life and death. Believe me I have visited each and everyone one. I have decided visiting is good enough. I don't want to live there.

When I find myself focusing on a specific thing about her death, I don't push it away. It's important to allow feelings and thoughts to come. Then I chose to seek out blessings that were a direct result of this tragedy.

For instance, my last conversation with her may not seem like a blessing, but it was. It was terrible I hung up the phone and our time ended full of anger and sadness. However, hanging up kept me from hearing much worse from my mom, this is a blessing. I prayed for her when we hung up and I asked my friend Teri to pray for her. If you believe, then you know this is a blessing. My prayer did not stop her from taking her life, but I prayed for her to be protected and that God would be with her. I know God was with her and protected her. My kids didn't see me cry from being yelled at by mom. However small they may be, the blessing list continues. I slept fantastic that night, which seems like a strange thing to mention. Still, I was about to face many fitful nights, waking my husband up as I cried in my dreams. I needed a good night's sleep.

I woke up in a home with a loving husband and my

beautiful kids. I have great friends, food, clothing, shelter and funds to go to the movies and out to dinner etc…..

This is how you get out of bed each morning after a loss. You count the blessings. When your eyes open in the morning and what is missing is screaming at you and the pain is suffocating, reach for the smallest blessing. I woke one morning longing to roll myself up into a ball and push away the world, but I thought about bread. That's right, bread. Then I thought about toast. Then I thought about how fortunate I was to have a toaster and a kitchen to put the toaster in. Then I thought about my home and that made me think about the laundry. Then I found myself thinking about how my son constantly leaves his underwear on the bathroom floor. Then I thought about my son. One by one I counted my blessings until one got me out of bed.

I use to work with homeless veterans. Many of them were elderly. I met a man with snow white hair and a long beard that looked like icicles hanging from his chin. All he owned he carried in a back pack. He resided under bridges and in make shift tents.

He had walked all over the country, but the years were catching up to him and being homeless was beginning to take a toll.

As he and I drove to a shelter he would be temporarily staying at until he could move into a home for veterans, he imparted some wisdom. He said, "My life has been hard. Mostly because of things I chose. But I've always been blessed." I looked at this man with a weathered face and filthy clothes and asked, "How have you been blessed?"

He smiled at me with a twinkle of tears in his eyes and said, "I've slept under some of the most beautiful skies you've ever seen. I've lost great friends, but I had great friends. And when my body got too tired and sick of me beaten it up, God sent me an angel. You are an angel."

This encounter taught me a lot about perspective. What I may take for granted is another person's reason to get up in the morning. Don't get me wrong. I'm not Mary Poppins. I often successfully avoid God and ignore my blessings. During these times there is always a faint knowing, I can't stay this way. The self indulgence begins to gnaw at me.

The despair is so much about me. To submerge myself in despair is the beginning of making God disappear and will lead, I am convinced to eventual loss of hope.

Diary entry; *It shocks me to think that as I write this page my mom has been gone for 1 year and 4 months, yesterday. I've been very sad the past few days. I have been thinking about her, likely because Valentine's Day is approaching and I always send her something on this day of love. I send her flowers or a nice card, just a little something to tell her that I love her. So, today I took a few hours off from work. I have napped, watched a little TV, collected eggs from the chicken coop and now I am writing. Its 5:00 and I only started writing a half hour ago. Avoiding the very reason I took time off from work, avoiding paying attention to the fact that I miss my mom. I miss her very much. Surprising in a way because I was so frequently uncomfortable around her. But, I did really like to make her laugh and I did like to tell her about the kids and everything they were up to. I want to tell her about Emily liking boys and about Sam shaving for the first time. I want to tell her about my trip to Las Vegas with my girlfriend and make her laugh with my tourist stories. So, the tears come once again. Will the tears ever totally stop?*

20

TALK YOURSELF INTO IT

"But he said to me, "My grace is sufficient for you, for my power is made perfect in weaknesses."Therefore I will boast all the more gladly about my weaknesses, so that Christ's power may rest on me. That is why, for Christ's sake, I delight in weaknesses, in insults, in hardships, in persecutions, in difficulties. For when I am weak, then I am strong."

2 Corinthians 12:9-10 ®NIV

My sister once said, "I wonder why I am where I am in grieving the loss of our mom and why you are where you are." I told her, I chose to focus on all that is good and true in my life rather than on mom's death. It is a purposeful task daily to turn my eyes, mind and heart elsewhere when I find myself thinking of her suicide. It is easy to become consumed with a loss. It is critical to find balance in grieving and not allow the loss to consume you. Some people have a tendency to believe if they start feeling better then it means they didn't really value what they lost. Like my sister said, "Sometimes I feel like I don't have the right to be happy." When she said this, all I could think, *you do not have the right to not be happy!* Letting loss over shadow all the grace and good that is in one's life is destructive not only to the person grieving but to those around who care about them. Marriages can fall apart, children can be neglected or worse bear the brunt of the anger and sadness a grieving person feels.

Self talk helped me a lot. You know yourself better than anyone. When you do not have the energy to get out of bed, talk yourself into it. For a long time after mom's suicide when I would wake up I'd count my blessings and then self talk, "You can do this. Don't fade away. Do not allow this to take you down. Get up and face the day. Show your kids it is possible to make it through a tragedy. Get up!"

Think of anything you have done that took courage. Throughout your life you have self talked to conquer something. For some it was as big as jumping out of an airplane. For others it is having the courage to speak publically. This is not different. You have to have courage to face each day and ultimately it is your decision. So talk yourself into it.

Visualization was also very helpful for me. When a person has lost something or someone particularly to suicide we have a normal tendency to see an image of that person dead.

Some have a picture in their head because they actually found the person and others because their imagination gets the best of them. Whatever the circumstance, many tend to replay the most awful parts over in the memory. For days I found myself continually shocked by the images that would pop up in my mind about what my mom must have looked like. Trying to rest was the worst because everything was so quiet. It was just me and my mind and without effort the disturbing images would pop up. I would feel sick and afraid. Then one evening when I was trying to rest I closed my eyes and before my mind could take me to places I did not want to go I took it to a place I did want to go.

I visualized myself resting in a beach side bungalow. The crisp white curtains snapping in a gentle breeze lulled me. I was lying on a big fluffy bed listening to the ocean.

I could hear footsteps on the dock and opened my eyes to find my husband casually standing there with the corners of his mouth lazily curved up. He looked so handsome. His skin tan making his blue eyes stand out. He wore khaki pants and a white linen shirt. He came in and snuggled up next to me on the bed…I drifted off to sleep. I woke up the next morning in our house and in our bed.

I found myself visiting this place often for several weeks. I would also visualize my mom. I would picture her looking beautiful, rested and happy. I could see her perfect smile and my heart would be at ease. This is how I want to remember her. This is how I choose to remember her. Doing this saved me from going to terrible ugly places in my mind and helped me to rest….eventually.

Talk to your friends. Friends are a rope to reality. They will cry with you, pray with you and when you're ready they will laugh with you. Friends can be a phenomenal distraction or patient listeners. My friends reminded me daily that everything I felt was normal. They encouraged me to extend grace to myself. When I knew they must be so tired of me and my circumstance they would take my hand, sit me down and tell me that they will never be sick of loving me. Friends remind us, we aren't meant to walk alone.

21

TRUST IN THE LORD?

"And we know that in all things God works for the good of those who love him, who have been called according to his purpose"

Romans 8:28 ®NIV

Honestly, in my very human way I keep thinking that such a monumental loss should be compensated with something equally as great. I cling to Romans 8:28. In my very human perspective I want the good to be as good as the bad was bad. It is easy in this life, being in this world to focus on what I want not what I have. I have multiple blessings from this tragedy; the biggest is a pure knowing that God is with me. His whispers have been mighty. *Oh Lord! You have been such strength, such a good friend.* I'm ashamed to admit I can feel sometimes like this gift is not equal the tragedy. I force myself to think on every moment with God since my mom died. I focus on each whisper that has comforted me or pushed me forward.

I have had wonderful visits with people who are grieving a loss. I feel I am able to mirror hope for them. This feels good. I sense that in the big scope of my life, maybe with time the great will be equal to the tragedy. The time I have with God, the whispers I get to hear and the people I can touch. Perhaps the sum will be great if I look beyond my own nose. It happens to people repeatedly in the Bible. They went through terrible things never to see the full impact their story had on the world. For example, Job never got to meet me! Job had no idea he may one day; thousands of years later inspire a woman to trust in the Lord.

So, I trust in God. I find comfort and even joy. I wonder if someday, hundreds of years from now someone could be inspired by my story. If they chose to hear God's words as they struggled to keep from drowning in their sorrow. If they chose to be hope defined, would my pain be worth it?

Just dreaming of a moment like that somewhere in the future makes me feel wonderful peace.

Even with His presence being so apparent to me through all this and His voice being so reassuring and loving at all times, can I fully trust the Lord again? How do I not live in fear of the millions of bad things that can happen? The chaos of our will colliding with his perfect will. Tragedy is often made up of imperfect free human will. The answer is to surrender. Nothing can hinder God. He can and He will restore you. Choose to trust.

I'm not suggesting it's easy, but it is simple. Surrendering to God completely, giving everything over to Him; pain, anger, shame, all of it! Crying out and acknowledging His steadfast presence and power, your weakness and His strength. Treat Him as real as any other person you can see with your eyes. Wrap yourself into a relationship with Him by studying His word and by praying. Then you will know His heart. The trust will come.

22

FAST FORWARD

"You will be secure, because there is hope; you will look about you and take your rest in safety."

Job 11:18 ®NIV

It's been five years. Emily and Sam are much older and have been told the entire ugly truth. The truth haunted me. I knew they had to know. We are a family that talks about everything. I did not want a monster hiding in the closet. My heart raced as I spoke the words, "grandma shot herself." They both felt anger, but they also understood why we did not share this detail with them. Emotions spilt out and we held onto each other.

Sam went directly to his room and put on a jacket my mom bought him when he was about seven years old. His six foot frame crammed into it, with the sleeves barely reaching his elbows. He had a lot of questions. He cried off and on through the evening. I do not think he will ever be able to part with that jacket.

Since he found out the truth questions have come sporadically. He gave a talk at his youth group about faith and how this loss brought him closer to God. As it turns out the moose story is profoundly important to him. God showed up for him that day as much as He did for me.

Sam says what his grandma did caused him to be very sad. However, he also says, "I'm in a good place mom. My walk with God is strong. I think I can be a light in other peoples' lives."

Emily's reaction was as most emotional things are for her at first, logical. If she were a movie character she would be Spock. She said, "Well, I wish you would have told us the truth from the beginning, but I get why you didn't. And she is dead, she killed herself so I guess how she did it is irrelevant."

She had a few questions. She expressed sympathy for me and even more for my step father Bill. She grieves in subtle more calculated ways. She frequently walks to the cemetery. She writes music and poetry.

Thankfully, they both seem to talk when they need to and ask questions when they have them. Hope is an important word in their lives. They are kids burdened with a terrible tragedy, but as a result are strong, insightful and loving. They are phenomenal people.

23

SPECIAL DELIVERY

"But ask the animals, and they will teach you, or the birds of the air, and they will tell you; or speak to the earth, and it will teach you, or let the fish of the sea inform you. Which of all these does not know that the hand of the Lord has done this?"

Job 12:7-9 ®NIV

Emily and I participated in a Christian theatrical production. We portrayed ourselves and disclosed a commandment we have broken. My commandment was, "Thou Shall honor thy father and mother." I reenacted the last time I saw my mom, the day I told my husband, "I wish she was dead." Opening week was demanding. Sharing how I spoke about my mom with an audience loomed over me. I prayed daily, "Lord God let me honor you. I do not want to dishonor my mom. I pray someone will be blessed by what I am about to share."

Opening day I woke with anxious anticipation. As I hurriedly got ready for the day I heard my husband shout, "Leslie you need to get out here, hurry!"

I ran to the kitchen and saw my husband standing at the back door with a huge smile on his face.

"You are not going to believe this. Come here."

There in the backyard was a moose, the second moose to grace my life. I stepped out onto the deck and watched as it danced in a circle.

"Of all the days' sweetheart, is it just me or does that moose look like he's thinking; 'What the heck am I doing here!' I think this is meant for you." With that Pat went inside.

I stood there in awe and watched as the moose lazily drifted into the trees. I felt completely insignificant and so significant at the same time. With tears streaming down my face I lifted my hands to heaven and whispered, "thank you."

Two hours later Emily pulled out of the driveway to go to school. As she headed down the road the moose stepped out of the trees and in front of her car. It stood there long enough for her to take a picture of it with her cell phone.

Seconds later she sent the picture to me with this message, "OMG! I almost hit a moose. I think this is a good sign."

God is so good.

24

HOPE

"May the God of hope fill you with all joy and peace as you trust in him, so that you may overflow with hope by the power of the Holy Spirit."

Romans 15:13 ®NIV

HOPE DEFINED

Diary entry; Hope is an amazing thing. I'm looking outside my window right now and can see spring is starting. The sky is gray teasing the ground with rain that is soon to come. I can see the tips of crocus emerging. There are a few buds on the trees and the wind is warmer than it has been. I feel restless to plant something. Soon the brown grass will be green and the vacant tree limbs will be full of leaves. The black birds will arrive and start singing their haunting tune. Then the robins, finches, kill deer, sparrows and hummingbirds will be fluttering all around. Everything that appears to be dead will be reborn.

Hope is written on the very grass I walk on. If I pay attention I can hear hope being whispered in the wind. It is a gift. He masterfully courts me with the seasons and shows me there is hope even in a withering flower. As His *child I am hope defined.*

For more information on Leslie Stickel or to purchase
Hope Defined products, please visit;
www.hopedefined.com

LaVergne, TN USA
18 April 2010
179571LV00002B/5/P

9 781432 753344